Sultry

A lip-biting, heart racing collection of poetry and prose that's written to tease

r. A. bentinck

FYAPUBLISHING | GEORGETOWN

FyaPublishing
95 South Turkeyen,
Georgetown, Guyana.

Sultry **r. A. bentinck**
ISBN **978-0999444566**

Cover design by **r.A. bentinck**
Cover image by **D'Andre Kirton**
Model: **Dhalia**

Psssst…

The seductive tease, I can assure you, will be exquisite…

—r. A. bentinck

entinck

Always with Love

CONTENTS

Preface 9

Wet Words.. 11

Sweet Talk You 13

Drenched 14

Sweet Whispers 15

Walking Away.. 16

The Pictures... 17

Nibbling.. 19

The Kissing Recipe.. 21

Probing for Honey 22

Rainy 24

Oxygen 26

Parting 27

Heavenly Hands... 29

Embrace... 31

With Time... 32

Get Use to This... 34

Time... 36

Fiery... 37

The Ease in Her Tease 39

The Mysteries of You 40

Wondering 42

Inseparable 43

Morning Thoughts 44

Kissology (the anatomy of a kiss) 45

Take Me There Again 47

Mornings of Memories 48

The Wind and Your Hair 49

The look of love 51

Starvation 52

Forgive Me 53

Those Eyes 55

Let Go and Let it Be 56

Expressive Eyes 57

My Secrets 58

Tonight 59

Just Surrender 60

Stay a Little Longer 62

This Moment 63

How I Want You 64

Waking Up To You 65

Sultry

Running Around 66

Right Now 67

Tomorrow 68

Heart on the Line 69

Fluids 70

Obedience 71

The White T-shirt 73

Beautiful 74

Lost in the Moment 75

Do It Again 76

Afraid 78

Can't Get Enough 79

Forgetfulness 80

Playing with Her Fire 81

Take Off Her Clothes 82

Sensual Vibrations 84

She is the Reason 86

When I Say... 87

You're My Poetry 90

Connecting Spots 92

Daydreams 93

Is This Really You?.. 94

Just One Moment... 96

Listen.. 97

Seducing You 99

The Taste of You... 101

Smouldering 103

Stealing Breaths.. 104

It's You and Me Tonight 106

My Love 108

My Inspiration 110

Acoustic Love.. 112

Sunrise.. 113

Poolside Beauty... 114

Sweet Sensations 116

Indescribable 117

Sleepless 118

Overthinking.. 119

On the Cheek 120

Hard to Get 121

A Ballad for the Broken (to My Sisters with Love) 122

Closer.. 125

Don't Go.. 126

Sultry

A Little Longer 128

Hush.. 130

Cornered 132

Remembering 133

I Won't 134

Not a Player 136

Sitting and Watching (Egotistic) 138

Oohs and Ahs 140

Heartbeat 141

On the Dance Floor 142

A Sweet Discovery (for Neelam) 144

The Passing Smile 146

Caged Scream.. 147

Bliss 148

Comfort Zone 149

Connecting Dots 150

Ember 151

Embrace.. 152

Sipping Her Lips... 153

Footprints... 154

Her Hands.. 155

Her Memories 156

Hostage 157

How? 158

Hummingbirds and Bees 159

If I Follow 161

Infliction 162

No Comparison 163

Paradoxical 164

Fantasising 165

Cravings 167

Feast on Me 168

Indecent Proposal 169

Intentions 170

Flirty 171

Night Lights 172

Reservation 174

Unplanned 175

Woman Enough 176

The Dirty Looks 177

Playful Lips 178

Wanting It All 179

Playful Torture 180

Sultry

Beautiful 181

Close to You 182

Earth Angel 184

The Reason 185

After You 186

In My Arms (T.L.C.) 187

The Taste of Love 189

Your Fire 190

You Are the Reason 191

There is a Reason 192

When You Smile 193

Dewdrops 194

Watching 196

Wordplay 197

Seduction Knocked 198

Pillow Talk 199

You Are Too Close 200

Under the Stars 201

Skin to Skin 202

The Closer I Get 203

Let Me 204

In-between Time.. 205

Desperation.. 207

Overly Excited... 208

Reading Me 209

Salacious Appeal 210

About The Author... 213

Sultry

Preface

"Sultry: A lip-biting, heart-racing collection of poetry and prose that's written to tease" is exceptional storytelling in the form of amorous poems. The poet speaks directly to the reader's heart, mind, and fertile imagination. I guarantee every piece in this book will evoke some kind of emotion from the readers.

This collection celebrates love and intimacy in a refreshing and compelling way. Bentinck uses sensual metaphors, erotic imagery, and other poetic devices in an enticing way that transports the readers on a refreshing sensual journey. There are pieces on topics ranging from the first sensations of lovemaking to intense, unbridled lust, the longings of horny lovers, and erotic fantasies. You will definitely experience something when you peruse this collection. Whether it's joy, happiness, sensual gratification or curiosity.

This compilation of poetry is a celebration of the varied and intricate emotions associated with intimate relationships. From intense and passionate cravings to seductive passions.

The poems within this collection will not only, tease and please you in a variety of forms, but some pieces will help you celebrate and recognise the healthy connection between sexuality, intimacy, and the connecting of hearts.

Georgetown,
November 2019

r. A. bentinck

Sultry

Wet Words

there is something about
your endearing words
that makes me wet.

they turn me on like
a running pipe, and
get me so sexcited.

your poetic dexterity
leaves me weak
in the knees.
have me steaming up
in my clean clothes,
swiftly activating
the freak in me,
making my elegant dress
falls slowly
to the floor.

i get wild with excitement
at the thought of experiencing
the reality of your every word.
there is something about

those descriptive words of yours
that makes me wet.

something about your powerful
imageries that ignite a fire
in this fertile mind,
your words turn me on
like a pipe.

what are you trying to do to me?
can you fulfill
the promises in your every word?
can you satisfy my wild and freaky side?
can you tame these raging emotions
before it gets crazier in my mind?

Sweet Talk You

may i have a moment
of your time?
i want to sweet talk you.
i want to tell you
about the joys you bring me.

may i speak to you
away from prying eyes?
i want to sweet talk you.
i want to tell you how much
you mean to me,

may i have a few minutes
of your precious time?
i want to sweet talk you.
i want to sit in
the company of
your radiant smile
and tell you stories while
i get lost in your angelic eyes.

may i have a moment
with you?
i just want to sweet talk you.

Drenched

i am drenched
with desires for you.
you showed me a snippet of
your sweetness and now
i'm left with uncontrollable longings.
i am drenched
with desires for you.

your irresistible blessings
keep toying with me,
you test my self-control
and logical reasoning daily
i am drenched
with desires about you.

i am drenched
with your tantalizing tendencies,
your butterfly gaze,
your sugary smile,
your graceful walk
and your tranquillizing voice.
i am drenched
with insatiable desires for you.

Sweet Whispers

my lips to your ears
whispering the sweet secrets
you long to hear.

my lips to your ears
saying all the tasteful things
you want to hear.

my lips to your ear
whispering slowly
while i smell
the delightful fragrance
of your hair.

my lips to your ears
telling you
the pleasing things
just to light up your
bright and graceful smile.

Walking Away

there is something
mesmerizing
about her
when she gracefully
walks away.

her tender feet
romance the pebbles
on
the dusty road,

her hip sways
to the gentle music of
the whispering wind,

and she leaves
a tantalising trail of her
enticing fragrance
along the way.

she makes me
want to ask her
to stay a little longer.

Sultry

The Pictures

she sent me her pictures
today
and my descriptive engines
got turned on:

she oozed sensuality
in endless ways,

she was a refreshing
breath arresting beauty,

she looked
stunningly gorgeous,

she was the delicious
candy of my eyes,
she was the heat
in my consuming flame,
she caused the lust
in my burgeoning desires,
and the icing
on my easy-going day.

she sent me her pictures

she sent me her pictures

today and it was
the sweetest surprises
in so many ways.

Nibbling

i nibbled on
her earlobes and
she erupted
with steamy passion.

i can feel
her quivering body
begging for more,

i could see her body
contorts in the heat of
the moment's flame.

so i nibbled on
her earlobes some more
and her body
became overheated with
insatiable desires.
i deliberately nibbled on
her earlobes just
to stoke the fire of
her inner consuming lust.

i nibbled

and
nibbled
and
nibbled
just to taste
her sweetness
with my lips,
and exploring tongue.

The Kissing Recipe

- one ounce of
willingness,

- add tender touches to taste,
an unlimited amount of
lips and tongues.

- a dash a wild imagination
and a sprinkle of
lust filled desires.

- the soft closing of
the eyes are preferential.

- add a healthy dose
of tongue wrestling skills
and a small portion
of courage to be
fully involve in
the ensuing friendly battle.

mixed all ingredients
to personal taste and satisfaction.
bon appétit.

Probing for Honey

i was the persistent honeybee
who instinctively knew
what she was concealing
behind those tightly sealed lips.

so i probed and prod
with my exploring tongue.

i gentle kissed and smacked
her lips but
her steel barrier teeth
didn't make it easy for me.

so i invoked
my persuasive qualities.
i begged and i pleaded,
i coaxed and i cajoled,
i stayed patient and calm
throughout the initial ordeal.

her petal lips encouraged me
along the way,
her enticing fragrance
enflamed my senses
and kept me motivated.

Sultry

then after countless
probes and prods
she relented.

oh, the emotions that followed.

her honey aura was more
than i imagined,
her lips were softer than soft,
her tongue was simply magical,
and the sensation of it all
was euphoric.
she gives me a taste of
her honey flavours
and left me with
a sugary high.

Rainy

it's raining
but that doesn't mean
a thing.

we will sit
right here and
get soaked.

soaked
by the raindrops,

soaked
by our drizzling passion,

drenched by
the deluge of irresistible desires.

it's raining.
so what?
we are not going anywhere.

we will stay right here
and get soaked in
the downpour of
this moment's emotions.

Sultry

at the end
we will be wet,
but
aroused to
the sweet taste of
our closeness,

aroused by
our body heat,
and
aroused by
our irresistible blessings.

Oxygen

if it's not oxygen
why do i feel like
i'm going to die without it?

it's not like oxygen
but it feels like
i cannot survive without it.
if it's not oxygen
why i'm breathless
and suffocating?

it's not like oxygen
but i'm struggling
to breath without it.
i'm craving
your sweet lips against mine,
i'm craving
your warm and comforting caress.

it's not oxygen
but it seems like i need
your succulent kisses daily
just to stay alive.

Sultry

Parting

time invariably
finds a way to fly
when we are together.

time spent together is
delectable.

we are always
too caught in
the moment's beauty
to see when time
passes us by.

too wrapped up
in each other's presence
to pay attention to time.

until we meet again
i will hold your memories
close,
i will cherish the moments
shared,
i will savour
your every touch,

every embrace,
every word we shared.
our partings are always
bittersweet because
the flying time always
finds a way to leave us yearning
for more time
to be together.

Heavenly Hands

she willingly gave me her hands
today
and my whole world changed.

her hands felt like
the soft petals of a rose
and they smelled like perfume
from the sweetest of flowers.

she tenderly touched my cheek
today
and rearrange
my inner world.

her gentle hands were
my soft cloud,
my comforting pillow,
they were much more
than i imagined.

i gentle held her hands today
and my world will never
be the same again.
she offered me her hands

and they stole my heart away.

before today i never knew
holding someone's hands
could be this breathtaking
but
when she gave me her hands
today
she opened up
a whole new world for me.

Sultry

Embrace

it felt so good
to finally feel
her body heat.

her warmth satiated me
on a cold evening.

the gentleness of
her touch sends
bolts of enticing electricity
seeping through my
excited body.

her magnetic fingers
slowly massage me
and a soothing and
desiring sensation
accompanied her every touch.
her breath of longing
caresses the raised pores
on my neck. and something
about this entire moment
makes me weak to
all of her sweetness.

With Time

given time
i have gradually come
to realise
the inherent sweetness
that lies beneath
her masked exterior.

she knows how
to
delight and tease me.

she knows how
to flirt skillfully
with juicy words
that toy with me
in strategic places.

she knows when
to flash that alluring smile
while glancing slyly at me
with gentle eyes
that strip away all
my formidable defenses
and my sense of
moral rightness.

Sultry

given time
she has grown on me,

she mesmerizes me,
she entices me, and

the mention of her name
leaves a sweet taste in
my mouth every time.

Get Use to This

there will be
nowhere to run
and
no way to hide.

let your body
get used to this,
allow your body
to get used to me.

it doesn't matter
if you understand
why we met
and
why we feel
the way we feel
for each other.
let your body
get used to this,
allow your body
to get used to me.

don't be afraid
because it's
our first time.

Sultry

let your body
get used to this,
allow your body
to get used to me.

even if
you don't know how,
i'll show you.

let your body
get used to this,
allow your body
to get used to me.
it doesn't matter
where we are
the feelings will
remain the same.

let your body
get used to this,

allow your body
to get used to me.

Time

time has a malicious way of
slipping away when
we are together.
time seems to lose
its value when we sit
in each other's company.
time seems to gain tremendous value
when we are lost in each other.

it's astonishing how
we consistently lose track of time
whenever we speak.
with the wink of an eye
five and six minutes swiftly
turn into five and six hours.
every time we meet and speak
we invariably find ourselves
silently begging for more time,

wishing for more hours in the day,
afraid to look at the clock,
wanting more and more of
each other's company and warmth
while vanishing time nips at
our need to be together.

Sultry

Fiery

her coy exterior
is extremely deceptive,
she hides a bouquet
of sensual beauty
beneath it all.

her pleasant demeanour
is misleading.
she is a lot fierier
than i expected,

but in her fire
i wish to burn.

her stimulating imagination
can fondle your mind
in unimaginable ways,
her smile is inviting
and her eyes toy
with your delicate senses.

her selective words
take you to forbidden places
where you know its

wrong to indulge
but you have
no intentions of being right.
i am enticed by her fire.
like a moth,
i want to dance in
the heat of her flame.

she is so much fierier
than i expected,
but i don't mind
burnin' in her insatiable flames.

Sultry

The Ease in Her Tease

unconsciously she teases
with effortless ease.

the graceful flow of
her tantalising body as
she featly walks away,

the consuming fire in
her penetrating stare,

the soothing sound of
her shy laughter
fondle with my ears.

she doesn't have
to do much to
quickly entice,
gently tease,
stealthy seduce
and
to naturally stimulate
the pleasurable excitement
in me. she does it all
with unconscious ease.

The Mysteries of You

i am lured by
the mysteries of you.

i want to know what
makes you smile so sweetly.

i want to know the thoughts
behind those penetrating looks
you give me frequently.

i am caught up in
the mysteries of you.

i am tempted by
the mysteries of you.

tell me what
turns you on,
tell me all
about your guarded fantasies,

tell me what makes you
quivers with unquenchable desires.
i am enraptured by
the mysteries of you.

Sultry

i am enticed by
the mysteries of you.

show me what fuels
your passionate yearnings,

show me the way to
your seductive sanctuary,

show me the way to
your secret sweet spot.

i am enthralled by
the mysteries of you.

<u>Wondering</u>

i often wonder
what is going through
her mind
when words are
no longer useful

and
our breath
and
fingers speak
about what we are experiencing.

i oftentimes wonder
what's going through
her head when
she gives me
that indescribable look
which sends my emotions
on an instant high.

Inseparable

it's very arduous
to separate her
from
the joyful moments
of my days.

it's impossible
to go through the day
without something
reminding me of
her heavenly goodness.

she is an integral
part of all
my daily smiles,
my frequent laughter,
my blissful moments,
my countless inspirations,
and
my endless blessings.

Morning Thoughts

it feels so good
waking up to
morning thoughts
of you.

thinking of
your charming smile that
melt my heart,
reflecting on your silly grin
when you are cheerful,

thinking about
your luscious kisses
and your irresistible lips,

contemplating the warmth of your
comforting embrace,
considering the hypnotic sensation
of your natural fragrance.

it always feels pleasant
waking up to thoughts
of you in the mornings.

Kissology
(the anatomy of a kiss)

i get overwhelmed by
the amorous stupor
and
all my senses get activated
to this
one moment,
with these
multiplicities of sensations.

i watched her eyes
slowly close
and we drift off to
that place where
we began
to taste every flavour
on each other's tongue.

somehow i got to
the stage where
i could read
the messages in
her every breath,
where her hands

spoke a language too
complexed to be translated
into words
but
simple enough
for my body
to comprehend.

her lips were
invigorating,

her tongue was
alluring,

her breath was
soothing

and
the fragrance
from her hair was
enticing.

we were both
blissfully lost in
this kiss-filled moment
where our kissing appetite
became insatiable
by the minute.

Sultry

Take Me There Again

take me to that place
where our breaths
become one,

take me to that place
where our lips
get entangled in a battle
that doesn't involve
retreating,
nor surrendering.

let's go to that place
where our embrace
is so close that even
the wind can't find
a way through.

take me to that place
where we don't need words
to communicate because
our body language
is so fluent that
interpretation is instantaneous
and all desires are satiated.

Mornings of Memories

there is nothing to compare
to waking up with
the fond memories
of her affectionate kisses
on my mind.

there is a freshness
that comes from reminiscing
about her delightful smile.

her morning memories
wake me up in
the sweetest of ways daily.

good morning,
morning memories.

The Wind and Your Hair

i enjoy the way your hair
take flight in the wind
obediently dancing
to every rhythmic beat.

i love the fragrance
your hair releases
to the command of
the whispering wind.

i appreciate the way
the sun finds its way
through each wispy strand
lending rich colour
to your clustered beauty
in every way.

i enjoy the way the wind
play those tender games
with your hair,

one moment it tenderly
toss a few strands
concealing your eyes

and
every now and again
enough strands
to obscure your entire face,
some strands are even
wise enough
to steal a kiss by
slipping through your lips.

i love the way you slowly
brush those disobedient
strands away with such
seductive ease.
i love the sight of your hair
blowing and flowing
in the wind.

The look of love

you often ask,
why are you looking at me?

what are you searching for?

are you trying to study me?

i look into your eyes
because i am in love
with the way
you look at me.

i look into your eyes
because i am in love
with the way
your eyes caress me.

i look into your eyes
because i am in love with
the vibrations that
embrace me
whenever you look at me.

Starvation

it's more than just missing
your sensually sweet kisses,
its more like
i'm starving.

if this is not
starvation
then please tell me
what is it?

you have me craving,
you have me day-dreaming,
you have me fantasing,
you have me reminiscing,

you have me starving
just because i yearn
for your kisses.
this is much
more than missing
your delectable kisses,

it's an emergency that needs
your immediate attention.

Forgive Me

please forgive me.
it was never my intention
to desire you this much.

forgive me, please.

i didn't know that
i would grow to
crave so much about you.

please, forgive me.

i didn't know that
your hugs would be
so warm and enticing,

i didn't know your fingers
would be this gentle and magical,
i didn't know your lips
would be this soft and irresistible.

i beg for your forgiveness.
it's not that i don't have self-control,
it's not that i would die without

all your goodness,
it's not like i cannot think of
anything else,
it's just too difficult
at this time to pretend
that there is so much
about you to fall in love
with
over and
over again.
please forgive me
my weakness at this time.

Those Eyes

they look at me
with such seductive tease,
your gorgeous eyes.

they caress me so tenderly
and so frequently,
your sweet eyes.

your eyes toys
with my emotions,
drives me up
against a wall of desires,

set my emotions afire,
leaves me with
insatiable desires.
those sensual eyes of yours.
you look at me in
so many expressive ways
and it doesn't matter
where or when you still evoke those
gentle feelings that take
over me.

Let Go and Let it Be

when will you let
yourself finally be free?

why won't you release
your bridled emotions?

what would it take for you
to give free rein to
your racy fantasies?

when will you leave
your fears behind and just be?

when will you let go
and be spontaneous with me?

let go of everything and just be.

Sultry

Expressive Eyes

her eyes are
very expressive.
with one look
she can undress me in public
in her uniquely sly and
inconspicuous ways.

with her words
she can lie but her eyes,
they never deceive.

her eyes can be
mischievously deceptive
at times they tell me stories
of her seductive thoughts.

her eyes seduce me,
her eyes tease me,
her eyes please me,
her eyes turn me on,
her eyes lead me on.
her eyes,
the things they can do
to my excited imagination.

My Secrets

will you keep my secrets?

please don't tell my friends
that i lose my common sense
whenever i'm around you.

don't tell them i'm in the habit of
begging for more and more
of your sweetness.

please don't tell them
i love the freak in you dearly.

don't inform anyone that i can't
seem to keep my eyes off you.

please don't tell them i'm
a glutton for your precious kisses.
don't even mention
that i'm a sucker for your
delicious tongue.

please keep my secrets
between you and me.

Tonight

i just feel like
chilling with you
all cuddled up
in my arms tonight,
while we count the stars
and listen to slow jams
playing softly in
the background.

tonight, i just want
to be with you
in that cool and
relaxing way

where the soft breeze
caress your hair
and i can feel
the warmth of your body
pressed against mine
and your aromatic fragrance
dances in my nose.
i just wanna be
with you tonight.

Just Surrender

let my caresses
transport you
to places you have
never visited before

all i'm asking you
to do is
just surrender, baby.

don't resist
your innate feelings,

don't bridle
your racing desires,

don't stifle
your troublesome yearnings.
just surrender.
let my caresses
usher you to the edge of
your insatiable hunger.

baby,
i'm pleading with you to
just surrender.

Sultry

why are you trying to conceal
those sensual feelings?

what are you afraid of?
why won't you
just surrender?

Stay a Little Longer

i cherish every moment
in your presence
but somehow
time never does us justice.

can you please
stay a little longer?

i enjoy the sound of
your laughing voice,
and i savour
the sweet warmth of
your affectionate embrace.

baby, please,
stay a little longer.

your kisses are priceless
and the gentle look in
your eyes i can't
seem to get enough.

baby, please
stay a little longer.

This Moment

i was never told
that this moment
would be so special.
no one told me
that your sweet kisses
came with a combination
of all the right ingredients.

your smooth and supple lips
were like honey
glazed with extra sweetness.
your tongue spoke
the ultimate language
of pleasurable satisfaction.
your hungry fingers
took hold of my sensitive skin
and i can feel all
the emotions that are overflowing.

i was overwhelmed
by the purity and passion
of the moment and
all, i could do was wish it lasted
for more than just today.

How I Want You

i want to feel you with
my hands in your hands
up against the wall
overcome with
inextinguishable emotions.

i want to hear your
loud moans and groans
because words are
too difficult to speak
in the heat of the moment.

i want you with your eyes closed
as you get lost in the
overpowering desires of
this moment.

i want you with your nails
sinking into my flesh
as it cries out for mercy
yet still not wanting you to stop.
i want you breathing
with fast and uncontrolled breaths
as your body wiggles
under the weight of these sensual sensations.

Sultry

Waking Up To You

i want to wake up
to the memories of
my fingertips still
drenched with your perspiration.
i want to wake up to
the sounds of the
morning bird and
the warmth of your body
blanketing mine.

i want to wake up
to the lingering aftertaste
of your tantalising tongue
still in my mouth.
i want to wake up
to the pleasant sounds
of your gentle breath
while i get lost watching your sleeping eyes.
i want to wake up
to your aromatic fragrance
caressing each morning
breath.
i want to wake up
with and to the memories of you.

Running Around

i caught you today
running around
in my restless mind.

you were leaving traces
of your irresistible memories
all over again.

i saw the glow of your face
as we get lost
in a passionate kiss,

i heard your voice whispering to me
words that put my heart
in a sensual spin,

i watched you running around
in my mind today
and the footprints you leave
have me yearning
for more of you.

Sultry

Right Now

all i want
right now
is to feel
the warmth of
your pleasurable lips.

all i want
at this moment
is to feel your tongue
slowly fondling
my mouth.

all i want is
to look into
your dreamy eyes and
get lost in
your tender stare.

all i want
right now is
to be with you.

Tomorrow

the day has just ended
and i am already thinking
about tomorrow with you.
today was a gift wrapped up in your
lovely memories
and i can't wait
until tomorrow to do
it all over again.

when the night's sky
blanket the atmosphere
i count the hours
with excited anticipation
waiting for tomorrow
to come as sleep comes
quietly calling
i surrender to its urges
falling asleep with you and
tomorrow on my mind.
the day has just ended
and as i drift off to sleep
there is a satisfying smile
on my face
knowing that tomorrow
we will meet again.

Heart on the Line

i lay in all out there
i am not holding back!
i have decided to lay
my heart on the line.

i have placed
my strong emotions
and weaknesses
all on your table.

i have declared
my amorous intentions
and i have shown you
the inside of
my flaming fantasies.
i have shown it all
to you.
i don't intend
to hold back my feelings,
i am placing it all
on the line
because i know the feelings
i have for you is true.

Fluids

the slow and consistent
build-up of bodily fluids
told the true story of today.

we were soaked
with perspiration and
covered in a surplus of
unbearable body heat.

exploding sensuous juices
overflowed and glistened
the already slippery surface
of our burning skin.

today we rode
the slippery slope
of some intense emotions
and i am still recovering
from the electrifying experience.

Obedience

when i gravitate towards
your alluring eyes,
like a moth to the flame,

it's not an obsession
it's obedience.

when i give in to the call of
your wild and passionate side
and i get carried away
by the moments,

it's not an obsession
it's obedience.

at nights when i can't help
but give in to the temptations
of your unforgettable memories,
it's not an obsession,
it's obedience.

when kissing your luscious lips
and always wanting more
and more,

and more,
of those precious kisses,
it's not an obsession,
it's obedience.

when caressing you
in an affectionate embrace
and i don't want to let go
too soon,

it's not an obsession,
it's obedience.

it's me being obedient
to all
that is ravishing
about you.

Sultry

The White T-shirt

she suddenly appeared
from behind the locked door.
clad in nothing but
a big white t-shirt.

there was something alluring
about watching her walk
with such effortless ease
in her favourite
big white t-shirt.

she had a broad smile
veiling her face and
her bare feet played
a tapping beat
as they romanced
the tarry walkway.
it was a sight to behold
an unforgettable one.
today i saw a seductress in
a big white t-shirt.

Beautiful

wake up beautiful,
someone is thinking
about you early in the morning
and it feels so good.

hello, beautiful,
someone is happy
to see you once again.

goodbye, beautiful,
someone will be
missing you when you are away
even if it's for a day.

goodnight, beautiful,
someone will be
missing you while you sleep,

someone will be dreaming
of you while you sleep,
someone will be wishing
for the morning
to come quickly just
to see all of your beauty
once again.

Sultry

Lost in the Moment

with glazed eyes,
anticipatory desires and
lips that quiver
with pleasurable excitement,
we surrendered to the urgings
of a consuming kiss.

our breaths became one,
as our lips locked
in a heated battle
fueled by our mutual longings.

your fingernails
clawed into
the cotton fabric
penetrating my sensitive flesh;
it pains in a strangely
desirous way.
your body began
to speak a language
that makes me want
to find ways to
satisfy you even more.

Do It Again

you know that thing
you did to me
with your tongue
the last time we kissed?
do it again!

you know the way
your fingers roamed
my body uncovering
and discovering
sensitive places while fueling
uncontrollable desires?
do it again!

you know that
soft desiring look
you always give me
just before we close our eyes
loss in a blissful kiss?
do it again!

you know that moaning sound
you make every time
the feelings get overheated
and you get carried away

Sultry

on an amorous cloud?
do it again!
all the things you do
to take my breath and
inhibitions away
just do them all over again.

Afraid

she warned me repeatedly,

baby, i am afraid to
let go of these
surging urges.

i don't think
i will be able to
control my emotions
when i am with you.

she paused then continued,

if i let go
i will pin you to
the floor and i won't let you getaway.

i am afraid for you baby,
this is all new to me
and i don't know
what will happen,

i am really afraid for you.

Can't Get Enough

it's hard to get enough
of you, when each day
you get sweeter,

each day there is more
to discover,
more to savour,
more to delight in,
more to celebrate and treasure.

it's hard to get
enough of you,
when every day
in every way
you get sweeter
and more irresistible
by the hours.

Forgetfulness

i backed her up
in the corner of
the room and
i devour her in
a deep and passionate kiss.
seconds felt like minutes
and minutes felt like hours.

she pulled me closer,
held me tighter,
she had me in a
vice-like grip
as the sensation
flooded her body.

her breathing
changed pace and rhythms
and her breath became warm.
when we slowly retreated
she looked me deep
in my eyes and said softly,
you made me forget
how to breathe,
you caused me
to lose my breath.

Playing with Her Fire

i can see the fire
in her eyes and
i can sense
the inherent dangers
of letting her in.

but i have the curiosity
of a child and
i want to discover and
learn more about
her seductive heat.

i want to play with
her flames.

so i let go and
let her in. it was one of
my boldest decisions yet
and every day
i get to savour her
in ways i didn't ever expect.

Take Off Her Clothes

she kissed me
tenderly,
she kissed me
deeply,
she kissed me passionately,

now i can feel my fingers
urging me to take off
all her clothes.

when her tongue
plays with mine,
when her lips
touches mine,

when we get
lost in a sensuous kiss,
and i can feel her breath
burning her intentions
on my skin
i can hear my fingers whispering,
take off her clothes.
every time she
kisses me tenderly,
every time she

Sultry

kisses me deeply,
every time she
kisses me passionately

i can sense my fingers
itching to take off all her clothes.

Sensual Vibrations

it's in your relaxed and
piercing countenance,

it's in the slow parting of
your luscious lips that curve into
an irresistible smile,

it's in the twinkle of
your eager eyes
as we drift away in
an exploratory gaze,

it's in the ease of
your body language
that toys
with my carnal needs.

i can sense your desire
to connect on a deeper level,

i can feel your need
to have answers
to the many questions
running around in
your head.

Sultry

 i can detect
your thoughts
slowly romancing mine.

i can perceive it all
in your sensual vibrations.

She is the Reason

she is the reason for my sweaty palms.
she is the reason for
my wrinkled sheets
and my shaking knees.

she is the reason for the fire in my loins,
she is the reason for
the beads of perspiration
trickling down my spine.

she is the reason for the smile on my face.
she is the reason for
the aching i feel
in my heart.

she is the reason why i sleep like a baby
some nights and
she the reason why
i am up late at night because
loneliness is giving me a fight.

When I Say...

when i say i love you
i am not talking about
the cookie-cutter kinda love,

when i say i love you
it means i will walk
with you on those
arduous days when
your feet hurt and
everything pains
in an uncomfortable way.

when i say i love you
i am not talking about
the kinda love that lust
off of your body,
i am talking about
a love that appreciates you,
body and soul,
where i take the time
to worship you and
your spirituality.

when i say i love you

it's not the selfish kinda love,
it's the kind of love
that allows me to know
when to shut up and
listen to you even when
i want to speak,

it's the kinda love
that allows me to sit
with you in your silence
as we listen to the
wisdom of
the whispering wind.

it's that kinda love.
when i say i love you
it means on cold evenings
when it gets extremely frigid
i will give you
the t-shirt off my back,

i will give you the warmth
of my skin and
i will embrace you
so close that
the chilly breeze will be
left out in the cold.

when i say i love you
i am not talking about

Sultry

the cookie-cutter kinda love,

it's love on a deeper level,
love on a deeper vibration,
a love that
will fight with you,
a love that
will fight for you
against your psychological demons,
against your forgettable past,

a love that will love you
beyond and despite
your faults and scars,

a love that will cherish you
just because you are you.

You're My Poetry

i get lost in
your racy rhythm
time after time.

you draw me in
with your seductive smiles
and i am seduced
by your similarities
to so much in nature.

you capture me
with your metaphors
and i surrender
to their endless temptation.

your imagery arouse
my senses and lead
me to wide-open fields
without no fences,
there my imagination
runs free.

i sail away with
your rhymes and
in a unique way

Sultry

they make me feel so fine.
i am overwhelmed
by your superb hyperboles
that embodies the essence of
you and me.

each day in so many ways
you are my daily dose of poetry.

Connecting Spots

my tongue gently
traces lines connecting
the all the sensitive spots
on your erogenous zones.
i do it with one objective
in mind,
savouring the sounds of
your exploding ecstasy.

my tongue searches
each raised pores
on the surface of your
aroused skin
looking for your weak places
to tease you
to the point
of no retreat.
i do this with
one objective in mind,
blowing the covers
off your inhibitions
and setting
your imprisoned desire free.

Daydreams

you are the fantasies
in my forbidden daydreams,
you are the fuel that ignites
the fire in my sensual soul.

when i am with you
i forget the world
and its troubles
while we drift away
in sweet ecstasy.
you are the fantasy
that takes me to places
i have never been before,

where no limitations exist
and i am free to be me.
you give me reasons
to ask for more:

more of what you give me,
more of what you bring to my life,
more of what we create together.
you are the main feature
in my eyes-wide-open recurring dreams.

Is This Really You?

is this really you?
are those your eyes
smiling back at mine?

is this you?
is this your tongue
wrestling with mine
with such effortless ease?

is this really you?
is that your
out-of-control breathing
that's warm against my neck?

is this you?
is this your hipbone
bumping and grinding
against mine
in unison to our sensual rhythms?

is this really you?
are you sure you are
the innocent soft-spoken
girl, i know?
all this time

Sultry

you were in front of me
i didn't see any of this
in you.

just before you go
i have one request,
can you grind
on me some more?

Just One Moment

all it takes is one moment,
one fleeting moment
when we choose to surrender
to the callings of
our ever blazing desires.

there is no better place
to be,
there are no better feelings
to feel,
there are no better sounds
to hear
than our sounds of satiation.

all it took was one moment
to take us away
on a journey
so sweet, so seductive,
so mind-blowing,
so pure, so filled with the
ideal chemistry.
all it takes is one moment
for us to take flight
on feelings so high
we can touch the clouds.

Sultry

Listen

i'm listening to the rain
on the tin roof
as it complements
this moment beautifully.

i'm listening
to our heartbeats
racing in tune
with the sounds we create
as we make love
all day.

our favourite music
is set on repeat
as we tuned in
to its rhythmic beat
and sensual lyrics.
listen to the rhythms
we make when
hips speak the same
language
and bodies wrestles
unrestricted.
listen to the music

we create as we savour
the essence of this
unforgettable moment.

Sultry

Seducing You

one of these days
i will sneak up from
behind you

while you are in deep
concentration
doing your work
and i will
fondle your apples
and
play with your cherries.

as usual,
you will
find a plausible reason
to stop me.
to interrupt my flow.
to slow me down
and
tell me to cool out.

but i in
my usually unique way
will find ways to convince

you to play along.

i will find a way
to make your juices flow,

i will find a way
to make you ask for more,

i will find a way
to make you say
with that hungry look
in your eyes…

DON'T YOU DARE
STOP NOW!

The Taste of You

you are beyond
irresistible.

you have
long gone pass
succulent.

you are more
like hot chocolate
drizzled with
extra honey-
sweeter than sweet!

you leave
an indelible
aftertaste in
my mouth
you keep my imagination
active.

your memories are
like strong coffee
that keeps me
up late at night.

you leave a flavour
so divine.
i am left with
a constant yearning
for more of you.

you are more than
satisfying,
you are more than
mouthwatering,

you are more than
a hunger.
you are more like
nutrients,

an exquisite meal,
a thirst-quencher
a long and satisfying glass
of cold fruit juice
on a sweltering
summer's day.

Smouldering

i am still feeling
the heat you left
in me from our last escapade.
i am still surrounded by
your sweet memories
every hour of the day.

i am still turned on
by your enticing imagery
and mind teasing ways.
i can still taste
the flavours of you
on the tip of my tongue.

i can still smell
the essence of you
in every way,
your scent still lingers
in the halls of my nostril.
i am still smouldering
from all the heat
you left on me
and with me
from the last time we met.

Stealing Breaths

the closer we get
the more sultry
we become,

the closer we get
the more enticing
the moments become.

somehow the way
you touch me
always manages
to slowly
steal my breath
away.

somehow the sensuality
of your touches
always finds away
to make me
lose control.

you take me to places
that makes me
want to stay
in

Sultry

your presences
in
an indefinite way.
the closer i get to you
the more i want you,

the closer i get to you
the sweeter
each moment becomes.

It's You and Me Tonight

tonight,
it's all about
you and me
under a blanket
of glittering stars.

tonight,
it's you and me
lying on
the convenient rocks
as our mattress
and a plump pillow.

tonight,
we will savour
the melodic music of
the whispering wind
and enjoy
each sweet and
welcoming caress.

tonight,
it's you and me
making music
as we dance to

Sultry

the distinctive sounds of
our soft moaning.
tonight,
we will get lost
in the gentle lullabies
of the splendid moon
as she slyly watches
over us with
glowing approval.

tonight,
we will give in
to our voracious urges
surrendering meekly
to what comes naturally.

My Love

i want my love
to be the place you
come to for comfort
when it all gets too
crazy out there.

i want my love
to be the rag you use
to dry your weeping eyes
when life pains you
in unexplainable ways.

i want my love
to be your shelter
from the relentless
storm when there
is no port in sight.

i want my love
to be the blanket
you snuggle up
under when it gets
too cold outside.
i want my love
to be the guiding light

Sultry

in your darkest hours
when you think
there is no hope left.
i want my love
to be a safe place
you run to.

My Inspiration

i pride myself in being
skilled in expressing myself,
to the extent that
i am seldom at a loss for words.

then you came
into my life
and all of a sudden
i am struggling
to find the right
combination of words
to describe the blessings
you bring.

now, all my poetry is
centered around you,
all my rhymes
are about you,
all my metaphors
celebrate you,
all my similes
enshrine you.

you stroll into my life
and suddenly

Sultry

all the inspirations
i ever needed,
i found in you.
you are the muse
that inspire my thinking,

you are the muse
that motivates my writing,

you are the muse
that is my everyday inspiration.

Acoustic Love

she serenades me
by playing on my emotional strings
with her tantalizing words,
leaving a satisfying echo
in the corridor of my ears.

she strums on the cords
of my desires
with her delicious tongue
saturating
my insatiable longings.

she makes me
weak in the knees
with her pulsating tease
that energizes
all of my sensual faculties.
she knows how to bait me
with her smooth and lyrical words...

she said to me,
let's make music
with our tongues while
our bodies grind
to the rhythm of our overheated strings.

Sultry

Sunrise

you are like
the sunrise teasingly
peeking over
the horizon line,

flooding the earth
with your
dazzling brightness,
poetic beauty,
and refreshing rays.

you are like
the sunrise tenderly kissing
the fertile earth
softly smiling with
a certain sweetness
instantly adding
your golden light
to the birth
of a new day.
you are like the sunrise
you shine
your unconditional love
for all to see and feel.

Poolside Beauty

her
magnificent smile
and
magical eyes
were
the fuel
that turned on
my sensual engine.

this
poolside beauty
had some
breathtaking qualities
that was complimented
by her
red two-piece bikini
and
playful personality.
her
tempting smile
and
tantalizing eyes
were the accelerator
that revved
my emotional engine.

Sultry

this
poolside enchantress
had some mind-altering qualities
that was so magnetising
you couldn't help
but surrender to
the urge to stare
for a prolong period.

Sweet Sensations

the delightful sensations
gently steered her
to the seductive sanctuary,

transporting her away
from her familiar
and dull comfort space.

gradually she surrendered
to the irresistible urges
of this sensual environment.

and one by one
her unfulfilled fantasies
were satisfyingly fulfilled.

his spicy words,
the choice wine,
the flowing water,
her wicked intentions,
and her seductive juices
that flowed generously
all contributed
to the satisfying look
plastered on her now glowing face.

Indescribable

if i genuinely knew
all
the pleasant words
in the comprehensive
english dictionary

i will still struggle
to find
the satisfactory combinations
to describe how exceptional
you looked today.

i was floored
by your regal elegance,
stimulated
by your sexiness,
captivated
by the graceful way
you moved and
genuinely impressed
by how effortless
your poetic beauty
brilliantly illuminated the room.

Sleepless

her memories,
they always find a way
to sneak into my dreams
waking me up,

leaving me
panting for elusive breath,
searching for fresh air,
and with a strong desire
to be in her presence.

my sleep
is frequently interrupted
by her steamy memories
toying with
my insatiable need
for the satisfaction
only she can bring.
she seems to always
find a way into my dreams
in affectionate and teasing ways.

Overthinking

don't
overthink it, baby,
just go with the flow.

don't fight
your genuine feelings
just open the door
to your alluring desires.

release
your fears and inhibitions
and let's lay it all out
on the floor.

don't
overthink it
you will ruin
our natural rhythms,
don't
overthink it
let's surrender
to the mutual hunger
that dominates the room.

On the Cheek

she reached out to me
with pleasant hands
and delicate but electrifying fingers
caressing my cheek affectionately.

indescribable sensations
pulsed through my veins
while instantly delivering bolts
of pleasurable emotions
awakening all of my repressed amorous wishes.

she leaned over casually and faintly pecked me
on my blushing cheek.

the tempting warmth
of her lush lips
entered my pores and core,
and a swift storm
of pulsating emotions
instantly seized my body
and i became vulnerable
to the desire to hold her close.
she has these mischievous and girlish ways
of making me senseless
with lustful desires to be with her.

Hard to Get

i quietly reach to the sky
with a sneaky intention
to steal the stars just for you
but you won't give me a try.

i started to count the grains of sand
on the beach just to impress you
but you won't give me
the time of the day.

i went to the well
with a teaspoon just to fill
your empty barrel
and even that didn't please you.
i walked a thousand miles
bare feet
in the sweltering heat,
on the unforgiven asphalt,

my scorched feet told
the real story,
still, you won't give me
your time and attention.
what must i do to please you?

A Ballad for the Broken
(to My Sisters with Love)

she is an earth angel
who carries her natural beauty
with effortless simplicity.

but they have hurt her
so she doesn't trust love
anymore.

sister, please come home to love.

someone smeared her innocence
in her tender years and squashed
the petals of her fragile flower.

now she is on a hurting mission
and
she will take no prisoners.
she doesn't care about love
and she doesn't want to be loved.

sister, please come home to love.
her trust in men
has been compromised
now she finds it hard to believe

Sultry

and give in to her natural feelings.
her sexiness causes the thermometer
to explode but her heart
is cold as below zero.

sister, please come home to love.

her hands are soft as a baby's cheek
but her caress is as hard
as greenheart wood.
she has been badly treated
and repeatedly molested
now she finds it too complex
to trust her tenderness.

sister, please come home to love.

her gentle tears struggle
to penetrate her steely eyes.
she has cried a thousand tears before
in silent places but always manages
to fake a smile for the world.
she is hurting daily
in places she rather not tell.

sister, please come home to love.
i stand in her pain
for a fleeting moment
and empathy hurts like a bitch!

but she carries this hurt daily
and often the painful memories
come calling, softly but brutally.
sister, please come home to love.
if my unrepentant brothers can
only see the deep and long-lasting
scars and pains they subjected
our sisters to
will they ever change?
will they rearrange their foolish ways?
will they ever open their eyes
to see?

brothers let's please help
our sisters come home to love.
please.

Closer

come a little closer,
i want to whisper in your ears.
i have some things to say
that i don't want the rest
of the world to hear.

i want to tell you about
the things i want to do with you
and the places i want to take
your imagination.

come a little closer,
i want to tell you about
my secret intentions,
my wickedest desires,
and how much you set
me on fire every time i see you.
come closer, i want to smell
your sweet fragrance,
i want to hold you close,
i want to feel your breath
on my skin and i want to squander
the time away in your sweetness.
just come a little closer.

Don't Go

baby, please don't go yet.
if you leave me now
my thoughts of you
would have me up all night
and loneliness will
give me a severe fight.

please, baby
don't go just yet.

baby, if you leave now
i will lose my mind
sitting in the dark
thinking about no one else
but you.

please, baby
don't go.
baby, please don't get
tired of me
asking you to stay
a little longer.

don't get tired of me
asking you to squeeze me

Sultry

a little tighter.
don't get tired of me
wanting more and more
of your celestial sweetness.

please, baby,
don't go just yet,
stay a little longer.

A Little Longer

give me the little
you can give me now.

i will take the peck
on the cheek,
instead of the marathon
kissing session.

i will take the short
but affectionate embrace
instead, of our usual
prolonged hugs.

i will take the gentle
holding of hands
instead of walking
hand in hand aimlessly.

but,
i am not prepared
to wait another day
to hold and kiss you,

i am not prepared
to lose another precious moment

Sultry

with you.
the periods of my life
when you are not around
feel like one big void, a chasm
that's impossible to fill,
it feels like an eternity.

somehow this feels
like we are moons away.
i am accustomed to having
all of you,
i am accustomed to having you
in your favourite places
and in your preferred positions.

baby, desiring you
is something i have done
so long
now it's a hard habit to alter.

please stay a little longer.

Hush

hush,
don't say another word,
hush baby.
your eyes are telling me
the whole story,
let me listen.

i can see your lust-filled
desires in your glistening eyes,
i can see your hunger
that needs satisfying,
i can read every thought
that you are trying
to hide.

hush baby,
don't say another word
i know just what i need
to do.
let me lead
and you just follow.

let me set the pace
and all you have
to do is keep up

Sultry

with me.
let me create the conditions
that is conducive to your
total satisfaction.

let me provide
the solutions for all
that i see in your
revealing eyes.

hush baby,
don't say another word,
i know just what to do.

Cornered

she stepped into the crowded room
and i silently exclaimed,
good god have mercy on me.

she rearranged my level
of self-confidence,
snatched the breath from
right under my nose
and instantly started up
a musical orchestra
on the walls of my chest.

her perfume captured me
in a way that left me
transfixed on her
in a ghostly daze.
when she stepped into the room
i was at the mercies
of all her royal splendour.
she was an angel
in stilettoes, a temptress
in silk fitted dress,
and the reason for
my now weakened knees
and scattered thoughts.

Remembering

my hands
they remember
what you felt like.

my eyes cannot
get rid of the essence
of your radiant beauty,

my nostrils
remember your irresistible
natural fragrance,

and

my ears still echo
with the soothing sound
of your capturing voice.

I Won't

just because
i could
doesn't mean
i would.

i won't
fall for
your sweetness,
no.
i won't
give into
your sultry ways.

i won't
beg you
to stay when
you are about
to leave,
i won't
think about
your loveliness
when i can't seem
to get any rest.
just because
i could

Sultry

doesn't mean
i would.
i won't
follow
your temptation trail,

i won't
salivate at
your dining table,

i won't
drool over
your dripping honey.

despite all
your irresistibility
i refuse to give in
to you and all
your immeasurable splendor.

Not a Player

no,
i am not a player.
never has and
never will be one.

but,
i do understand
your love language.

don't envy my fluency,
in the way i interpret
your every need,

don't begrudge
my smooth ways
it's just my natural way
of responding to
your countless blessings.

no,
i am not a player.
i never was
and never will be.
i am only an obedient
observer who is

Sultry

humbly responding
to your irresistible
love pheromones.
no,
i am not a player.
i am not into
playing any games.

Sitting and Watching (Egotistic)

i am sitting here
watching you
making a fool of yourself.

you know
i'm gonna get you
don't you?

quit the girlish games.

i will sit here
and watch you
run till you get tired,

i will be right here
waiting
when you have come
to realize that loving me
is the only way,
and has always
been the only way.
i'll be right here waiting
while you fight against
what you feel
so naturally.

Sultry

i'll be here to feed
your hunger,
i'll be here
to quench
your emotional thirst

i'll be
sitting right here.

i'll be right here
waiting for you
when love leads you
my way.

i'll be here
come what may.

how long do you intend
to run,
to hide,
to disguise,
to play
your silly game.

how long?

Oohs and Ahs

i have grown to
appreciate deciphering
her language of pleasure.

it's evident in
the sounds she makes
that speaks
of insane satisfaction.

her english tongue
get confused and
she resorts to speaking in
oohs and aahs as
a sign of
her pleasurable approvals.

Heartbeat

why does your presence
manipulate my heartbeat
this much?
one thought of you
and my heart gallops
like wild horses
running free.

why the anticipation
of holding you in my arms
send shivering sensations
throughout my body?

when your lips meet mine
my heart beats at a speed
that's unfamiliar to me.
when you are far away
my heart rate slows
to a sad and dreary rhythm
and my emotions run cold.

why does your presence
control my heartbeat
this much?

On the Dance Floor

she is courteous and respectful
in person.
the sweetest and most
charming personalities
to be around.

but when she gets
on the dance floor
she instantly mutates into
a sultry goddess.

her once petite
and decent waste line
become a gyrating and
grinding machine.

her rhythmic moves are flawless
and she drops dance moves
that makes your mouth water
and your loins boil
with fierce desires.

her expanding waistline speaks
a dance language that simple
to interpret but difficult

Sultry

to erase from the overactive mind.
she is a lady in daily life
but on the dance floor
she is a tantalising sensation
that leaves you weak
in the knees and
drenched with perspiration.

A Sweet Discovery
(for Neelam)

from nowhere it seems
she stumbled upon
my poetic words,
then she found her way
into my thoughts,
and finally into my literary life.

her pleasant countenance
is sweet and succulent,
the gentle vibrations
she exudes
elevate the spirit
and sets me free from
the chains melancholy.

her pictures scream
classy royalty,
her regal elegance
is a splendid sight to behold
and something to cherish
dearly.
we are separated by
seas and continents
but that's doesn't restrict us

Sultry

from generously sharing
mutual respect and friendship.
i wait for the day
to bask in the glow
of her dazzling radiance.

we might be miles between
seas and continents but
this has turned out to be such
a sweet discovery.

The Passing Smile

it was right there
in her
passing smile.

the irresistible allure,
the pulsating sensations,
the spine-tingling blessings,
the heartbeat elevators.

it was all there,
right there in her
passing smile.

Sultry

Caged Scream

her controlled persuasion
held me in
frozen anticipation.

her precise attention
to meticulous details
tease me to the edge of my
already frazzled self-control.

i am trying my best
not to explode.
her electrical fingers
shock me to the core
i am holding on for
dear life,
but i can only do it
for so long.

the ear-shattering scream
breakthrough the barriers
and the neighbourhood
is set alight by my exploding
sounds of satisfaction.

Bliss

the
lazy stroll
of
clouds overhead,

the
sweet sway of
your flowing skirt
in
the afternoon breeze,

your
wispy hair dancing
to the rhythms of the wind,

the
seducing ring
of your silky voice in my ear
makes this afternoon
so much sweeter.

Comfort Zone

nestled in the comfort
of your abiding memories
i drifted off in a reverie.

i slowly drift away
in the bosom of asleep
so soft and sweet,

with a smile painted
on my relaxed face,
sweet dreams,
here i come.

Connecting Dots

i have developed
the art of
connecting the dots
from her head
to her pinkie toe.

i know-how
to find the right routes
on her spine to generate
the ideal sensations.

i know how to draw
the lines between
her lips
and her hips.

i know the intensity
and the amount
of pressure, i need to apply
on each of her pleasure points.

i have become a skilled
dot connector
every time i am with her.

Sultry

Ember

the fiery screams
and
intense moans
have subsided finally.

the fierce flames
in our loins
doesn't blaze as intensely
as before.

our weary bodies
sprawled in
the after-effects of
dying seductive embers.

emotions smoulder
in the glowing ashes of
crumpled fabric.
we lay there
staring into each other's eyes
speechless but satisfied.

Embrace

i can feel the
magical vibes
instantly transferring
from her inner being
to mine.

her gentle hands,
soft and sensitive
write unspeakable
emotions on my
alert senses.

she clutches me
in an affectionate embrace
and
i can feel
the private thoughts
she's thinking
and i can tell
she wants me
just as much as
i want her.

Sipping Her Lips

i took a sip of
her wine and tasted
the irresistible essence of
her lips on
the rim of the crystal vessel.

in offering me
a sip of her wine
she inadvertently
gave me a taste
of her delectable lips.

with that single sip
i am left with an
instant yearning
to taste the real ambiance
of her soft and sensual
petal lips.

Footprints

i just love how
you leave
angelic footprints
and
dainty memories
in my life
every time we meet.

you tiptoe
with feather-like steps
in the hallways of
my mind
leaving traces of
celestial blessings
behind.

Sultry

Her Hands

she held my hands
and i felt complete.
the soft and gentleness
of her palm
said to me what
words could
never say.

she held my hand
while we sauntered
in the pouring rain
and
the essence of
her tenderness
seeped into my pores
saying,
things will never be
the same after today.

Her Memories

her pleasant memories
are like a thermal blanket
on a cold and frigid
solitary evening.

in a comfortable bed,
with unfavourable
plump pillows
for my company
i wander off to meet
her engaging and
unforgettable memories.

her fond memories
were like a sincere
and welcoming blanket
on a bleak and chilly
quiet evening.

Hostage

your teeth are holding
my tongue hostage.

in the excitement
of the moment
she lost control
and
you give in to
her primal urges.

suddenly biting me.

now my tongue is
the innocent victim
of your unbridled emotions.

How?

we got engrossed
in the moments and
time crept by,

we were trapped
in a bodily cocoon,
and
the only thing
that mattered was us.

how did the bed
manage to get this wet?

when did the pillows
fall to the floor?
what caused us to lose all
sense of control?

we both looked
at each other
with questioning eyes

but neither of us
had the courage
to say what we were thinking.

Hummingbirds and Bees

i wanna be like
the hummingbirds and
the bees.

i wanna develop
that innate sense
to be able to savour
the sweet bounty of
your glorious nectar.

i wanna be like
the hummingbirds and
the bees.

i wanna be saturated
in your pollen
taking your aromatic fragrance
with me everywhere.
i wanna be like
the hummingbirds and
the bees.

i wanna be skilled enough
to extract your delicious nectar

without breaking
or smearing
your delicate petals.
i wanna be like
the hummingbirds and
the bees.

i wanna be the sole possessor
of the skills to access
all your precious sweetness
daily.

If I Follow

if i follow
my heart i will
fall for you.

if i follow
these feelings
i will fall head
over heels with you.

if i follow
your lure i will
lose my moral grounding.

but if i don't
follow i will
chastise me for letting you go.

Infliction

i was quiet in
my humble corner
then you came by
and
inflicted me with passion
so elevating.

you infected me
with a lust-filled disease
now am always
wanting more of you.

Sultry

No Comparison

i am trying to find things
to compare to the feelings
i get when i'm with you.

butterflies arrive
in abundance,
nervousness pays
an untimely visit,

temptations wouldn't
leave me alone.

nothing else can compare
to the things i feel
when i'm with or
around you.

Paradoxical

she forewarned me
in a stern tone,

i come with
my own complications.

i'm a good girl with
lots of naughty tendencies,
can you efficiently handle me?

i stood there
with a beaming grin
and a racing mind
wondering if i am capable
of handling
this apparent paradox
of a woman.
then
she disturbs
my thoughts process
with another question.
can you handle
all of this goodness?

Sultry

Fantasising

i will not lie,
i am fantasising about you
right now.

i am
looking at your full lips
and my thoughts are
taking me to places
where i can see you
do things to me
with those sexy lips.

girl, i am fantasising about you.

i see your curvy hips
and my desires pinned
me to the floor and
i can visualise
your rhythmic motions
as you bump and grind
uncontrollably.

baby, i am fantasizing about you.
i smell the uplifting scent

of your natural fragrance
and i drift away in a reverie
about you and me.
baby, i am caught up in
a fantasy about you
and it feels really good.

Sultry

Cravings

why do you
have to go now?
his inquiry interrupted
her teasing steps.

please stay
a little longer.

he pleaded with
desiring eyes and
an uncontrollable loin.

slowly,
she returned,
looked at him
with alluring eyes,
and butterfly kissed him
on the forehead,
then softly whispered,

i can't stay much longer
i have to go.
bye, sweetie.

Feast on Me

unleash your inner temptress.

throw away
your inhibitions
and let's get wild!

let your imagination
roam the undiscovered
sensual fields
and just feast on me.

open your eyes
and don't be shy,
see all there is
to see
and just feast on me.

Sultry

Indecent Proposal

are you afraid to eat it?

he stood there speechless
with a guilty
yet startling smile
plastered on his face.

nope!
(he was lying)
he replied nervously.

i want you to eat it
like an ice cream cone
on a hot summer's day,

she said with a face
flooded with confidence
and excited anticipation.
don't play around,
eat it like you want it,
eat it like you are starving.

Intentions

from the very first time
i laid eyes on you i knew
what i wanted
from you
and
what i wanted
to do with you.

my intentions
were vivid in my mind.

from the very first time
i held you close
in a friendly embrace
i knew what i felt
for you
and
about you.
my intentions
and feelings were
very clear.

i want all of you,
give me all of you.

Sultry

Flirty

She tightens
the screws
on her tease
and i pleaded to her.
i begged for more,
i asked her not to go,

i pleaded for her
not to stop,
i try to get her
to slow down

i told her not
to make so much noise.
then she intensified
the heat in her charm
and i was swarmed
by stinging emotions.

i am now a slave
to her unspoken temptations.
they say to me,
come get me,
please come take me.

Night Lights

the softness of the blue
disco lights clothed
your sensational curves.

Quincy Jones *'The Secret Garden'*
took control of our emotions
and we moved to the
commanding lyrics
and each seductive beat.

on a crowded dancefloor
you were the only one
i saw, you were the only one
i needed.
and as the lyrics took
hold of us
all i could hear was,
"i need to be with you
let me lay beside you
do what you want me to all night
gonna hold you, ooh baby, can i touch
you there"

we were both caught up in
the rapture of the moment

Sultry

and the dim disco lights
provided the perfect complement
to the smooth voice of Barry White's request,
*"tonight i want to learn all about
the secrets in your garden."*

Reservation

bartender,
turn down your lights
and pour my baby
a glass of fine red wine.

please put on some
Teddy Pendergrass
and leave us undisturbed.

this is a reservation
just for two.

bartender,
please turn down your lights
just a little lower
and pour my baby
another glass
of that special wine,
go on and leave us alone
this is a reservation for two.

Sultry

Unplanned

i didn't see this coming.
there is no way
i could have planned
any of this.

the slow burn,
the heat of the moment,
the fire in our eyes,
the insatiable calls
of wild desires,
the pleasurable sounds
and,
your kisses of ecstasy.

we didn't have what it
take to plan all of this
the way it turned out to be.
i couldn't see this coming.

Woman Enough

i don't want you
to be worried about me.

i'm woman enough
to deal with all that
you want to give to me.

don't hold back,
don't slow down,
don't go easy on me.

i'm woman enough
to take all you have
and can give to me.

don't be shy,
don't tell me any lies,
just give it to me straight.
i'm woman enough
to hear all
your nefarious thoughts.

give it to me,
i'm woman enough
to take it all.

Sultry

The Dirty Looks

she signalled
her wicked intentions
with a prolong
and intense dirty look.

she held me tenderly
by the hands
and tossed me
onto the welcoming bed,

and proceeded
to satisfy her
overwhelming needs
in a selfish way
that left me speechless.

Playful Lips

her rosy lips are
like licking
freshly spread butter
from a slice of bread-
silky smooth.

it's flushed and tender
like the petals
of dew-kissed rose.

when her pleasant words flow
you get lost in
the ineffable sweetness
of every word she says.

her lips have a way of
taunting you,
delighting you,
inviting you,
engaging you,

in ways that leave
you enthralled.

Sultry

Wanting It All

call me greedy.
call me a glutton.
call me covetous.

i don't care!
i desire all of you.

all your smiles.
all of your laughter.
all of your alluring smells.
all of your goodness.

call me greedy.
call me a glutton.
call me covetous.
i don't care,
give me all of you.

Playful Torture

i will torture you
slow and easy
with my pleasure tease.

i will take you
to the depths
of your rebellious
desires and release
you to the mercies
of their taunting.

i will take you to
the precipice of
intense pleasure
and expose your
vulnerabilities
and
i will be there
to fulfill all your
aching unfulfilled longings
and satisfy your need
to be pleased.

Sultry

Beautiful

your celestial gifts
merge beautifully
with your intellectual wit.

you turned on
your sunlight smile
and i'm enticed
by its ever-present rays.

you define
a rare kind of beauty,
one that few possess
and
many pray for.
you radiate natural beauty
effortlessly.

Close to You

it's the only place
i love to be
when i'm with you,

close to you.

it's the only way
i can smell
your aromatic fragrance
that puts me in a trance,

close to you.

it's the only time
i get the chance to
stare into your
gorgeous brown eyes
and get lost inside of your dream,
close to you.

it's the only moment
i get the opportunity
to bask in the glow of
your radiant smile,
close to you.

Sultry

being close to you
is the place i love to linger
for eternity and take in all of
your sweet blessings.

being close to you
is where i love to be.

Earth Angel

she protects herself
with an exterior
that is
fiery,

but beneath
the projected heat
lies her concealed gems.

eyes
that caresses you
so softly,
a smile
that seeps into
your heart
quietly lighting
it up with
unspeakable joys,
and
laughter that engages
your attention
in a way
that chases
your blues away.

Sultry

The Reason

you are the kind of girl
the stars come out for
on a lovely night.

you are the reason
the moon shines so brightly
in a clouded night sky.

you are the reason
the sun still shines
behind the gloomy skies.

and
you are the reason
why these days seem
so much longer and sweeter.

After You

after you kissed me
it feels like i've been
kissed for the first time.

after you made love to me
it felt like i made love
for the very first time.

when you touched me
the electricity that courses
through my veins
felt like i've been
touched for the first time.

after sharing
and experiencing
all of you
it seems like there
will be no one after you.

In My Arms
(T.L.C.)

in my arms is
where you need to be.

i wanna cradle
your passionate hunger
and fuel
your explosive fantasies.

in my comforting arms is
where you rightfully belong.

i wanna eliminate
your familiar fears
and fertilise the fields
for your unfulfilled needs
to grow.

in my protective arms is
where you should be.
i wanna embrace
your gentle warmth
and chase all
your blues away.

in my soothing arms is
where you should be.
i wanna taste
the ineffable sweetness
of your honey while
savouring the glowing embers
of your burning flames.

The Taste of Love

you are undoubtedly
what love taste like

you are precisely
what love feels like

you are genuinely
what love smells like

you are typically
what love sounds like.

in an unforgettable way
you embody
the true essence of
a natural love.

Your Fire

i am on fire and no one
can douse my flames
but you.

no one could have prepared me
for the heat generated
by your flames.

you burn me in places
i never thought
could be reached.

what is the source of
your fiery passion?

my quenchless desires
are consumed
by your eternal blaze.

You Are the Reason

it's because of
charming women like you
why sweet and happy
songs are sung.

it's attractive women
like you
that contributes
to the superb writing of
timeless love classics.

women like you
fuel the fierce fire of
erotic poetry and
sultry poetic language.

you are the prime reason
and the principal meaning
in every pleasant word,
every memorable line,
every soothing rhyme,
and every evocative imagery
in all my creations.

There is a Reason

it might be
the things that
you do
or
it might be
the things that
you say.

there is a reason
why i feel
this way.

your consistent effects
on me
keeps me
holding on,
keeps me
going strong,
keeps me
yearning
for you more.

When You Smile

when i see you smile
countless butterflies
take control of my body,
my imagination takes wings
and am enticed by
a multiplicity of feelings
that awakens in
the depths of my soul.
indescribable feelings.

when your lips
come alive my world becomes
brighter.
my countenance is elevated,
my eyes excited,
and am caught up
in the glories of you.

when i see you smile
you shine a light in
the atmosphere and
am enthralled by
the magical glow
and sweetness in your smile.

Dewdrops

i'm almost certain
your passionate kisses are
like dewdrops
resting on the petals
of early morning roses,

soft,
sensual,
irresistible,
and sweet.

i'm pretty confident that
those lips are
as gentle and tender
as dewdrops
slowly kissing
rose petals in
the early morning sunlight.
with lips so seductively alluring
they must feel like
drops of dew romancing
the tender petals
of a blooming rose.
with lips like those
even butterflies

Sultry

and hummingbirds
must be yearning
to taste their
honeyed sweetness.

i am a rose petal
you can be my dewdrop,
come lay
your affectionate kisses
on me.

Watching

you sensed my eyes
gently stroking you
from across the way
and
you intensify your tease
in every little thing you
said and did.

i knew you were aware
that i was staring at you
when you started
to ramp up your sensual meter.

my eyes now transfixed,
my imagination is in
a pulsing blender,
and my mouth is ajar
with extreme anticipation
as you slowly unleash
your fetching heat
bit by bit.

Wordplay

it's the way she gets lost
in her words when she
describe her sensual needs,

it's the way she closes her eyes
when her fertile imagination hits
her sweet spot,

it's the lingering yearnings
she leaves in the core of
your unsatisfied urges.
talking with her
is like having foreplay
with time to spare.

she has the perfect
word combinations.
she stimulates
the imagination and the brain
in unexplainable ways.

she knows what she wants
and she isn't intimidated to express
her feeling unashamedly.

Seduction Knocked

seduction knocked
and i opened but
i wasn't prepared for what
she brought with her.

she was draped with
the richest of blessings:
a smile that molested my
excited sensual senses,

eyes that snatch
my breath away
in an instant,

a touch that seeped into
to the core
of my insatiable desires.
seduction knocked
on my heart's door and
i opened up to her
and the unexpected excitements
that she brought left me
speechless.

Pillow Talk

the soothing sound
of your voice is
the perfect dessert
to the intense heat
of our love feast.

your revealing eyes
and your coy smile
doesn't paint a true picture
of your ravishing personality
beneath the sheets.

we are recovering from
an exhausting and
explosive session
of lovemaking by talking
the moments away
as we lay comfortable
and satisfied with each other's
sweaty company.

You Are Too Close

it's the only place
i love to be,
close to you.

it's the only way
i can smell
your sweet fragrance,
when i'm close to you.

it's the only time
i get the chance
to gaze into your
beautiful brown eyes and
get lost inside of
your dreams,
whenever i'm
close to you.
it's the only moment
i get the opportunity
to bask in the glory of you
when i'm close you.
you keep telling me
i'm too close to you
but it's the only place
i long to be.

Sultry

Under the Stars

as the evening gradually fades
our closeness takes on
a brand new meaning.
the mellow music in
the background guide our dancing feet
and fuels our emotions
while we danced under
the watchful eyes
of the twinkling stars.

i hold you close as we dance
the hours away,
i hold you closer and
i can feel your heartbeat
in sync with mine,
i can feel the rhythms of
your fluctuating emotions,
and i can smell the sweetness of your hair.

as the night swiftly fades
our closeness takes on
new dimensions
that brings us closer together.
and we get lost in the rhythm of romance.

Skin to Skin

there is
a certain magic
when we connect
skin to skin.

there is
explosive beauty
every time we exchange
bodily heat when we are
skin to skin.

there is
unexplained tension
every time your pores
wrestle mine
when we are
skin to skin.
the cares of the world
vanishes whenever
we are
skin to skin.

there is always magic
when we meet skin to skin.

The Closer I Get

the closer i get
to you,
the more i see
in you.

the closer i get
to you, the more i feel
for you.

the closer i get
to you,
the more i want
to be with you.

the closer i get
to you, the more i get
lost in you.

the closer i get
to you
the more at ease
i feel in your presence.

Let Me

let me take you to
the places you've never
been before.

let me open
the doors to your
undiscovered desires.

let me ignite the fire
of your smouldering yearnings.

and let me arouse
all your
secret fantasies.

In-between Time

until we meet again
everything seems
to last longer.

the hours
seem to drag on,
the days
seem like weeks,
and time slows
to a snail's pace.

in-between time
i think of you,

in-between time
i reminisce
about the glorious moments
we've shared,
in-between time
i crave you,

in-between time
i dream about you,
in-between time

i wish on a star
for you.
until we meet again
i will continue to
wish for time
to grow wings and
fly swiftly
until we meet again.

Desperation

she told me
i'm desperate.
desperate
for her to whisper
tantalising words
in my eager ears.
desperate for her to relax
and sync with
my sensuous rhythm and flow.

desperate for her to release
her sensual beast
on me and quench
my ever-burning flame.
she is correct
in all instances.

i'm desperate,
but if you see her
and step into my shoes
you won't blame me
for being this way,
because you will
get desperate too.

Overly Excited

maybe one day
you will come
to realise
why am so excited
by you.

maybe if you
just let go.

let go
of your doubts,
let go
of your fears,
and
release your uncertainties,

you too might be
overly excited just like me.
you give me reasons
to be overly excited
about you.

i don't have any apologies
for being excited
by and about you.

<u>Reading Me</u>

she has me figured out.
she can now
read me
like an open book.

she can sense it in
the way
i move,
the way
i speak,
and the way i laugh

that i have
an insatiable appetite
for her.

she knows i want
to taste,
and to explore,
all of her.
 and even after all that
i will still want
more and more
and more of her.

Salacious Appeal

she looked at him
with indulging eyes
and whispered:

i seriously wouldn't mind
if you just grabbed my face
and kissed me,
undress me slowly and
let your hands touch me
in places where your kisses
will soon follow.

without consent
his imagination galloped
to pleasurable places,
started witnessing things,
detecting sensual sounds,
and tasting seductive flavours.
she had the kind of eyes
that stimulated poetic verses,
while
triggering wicked intentions.
from the way
her eyes communicated
her message

Sultry

he could tell she wasn't
fooling around.
something about the way
she phrased her words
told him
she had gems in places
yet to be explored.

r. A. bentinck

About The Author

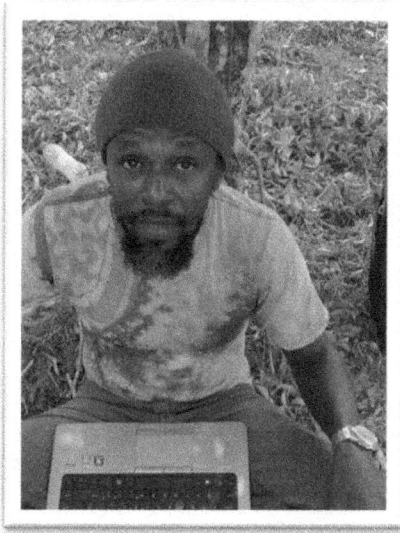

.r A. bentinck is the author of 7 other poetry books, including Of all the Lilies, Underneath the Poetry with My Girl, Underneath the Poetry and Bad Girl Stricken and Seduced. He lives in Georgetown, Guyana. His latest release, The Flaws in Our Teens, was a #1 bestseller in the Being a Teen new release category of on Amazon.

He is also an Educator and Artist who is focusing on his self-publishing business while tutoring part-time at the E.R. Burrowes School of Art as a painting and drawing Tutor. Bentinck is a graduate of the University of Guyana with a B. A. Degree in Fine Arts (Hons) and a Diploma in Education (Administration).